The League of Slow Cities

Armand Brint

Tenacity Press
Ukiah, California

To my parents
Shirl and Wally Grayson and Harold and Elaine Brint
who also live inside these poems

*Out beyond ideas of wrong-doing and right-doing
there is a field – I'll meet you there."*
Jalal ud-Din Rumi

Published by: Tenacity Press
P.O. Box 2710, Ukiah CA 95482; 1-800-738-6721;
write@openinginward.com

Library of Congress Cataloging-in-Publication Data
Brint, Armand, 1952
The League of Slow Cities / Armand Brint
p. cm.
ISBN. 1-892193-05-1 (pbk. : acid-free paper).
1. Poetry I. Title   2002
LCCN: 2002101000

Cover photo: Janet Wolfe Savides
Cover design: Theresa Whitehill, Colored Horse Studios
Printing: Morris Publishing, Kearney, Nebraska

Printed in the United States of America

Table of Contents

Jupiter Hall
(a child's mispronunciation of Juvenile Hall)

Driving down Clay Street,
my son turned to me
and said: kids shouldn't lie
to policemen
because if they do,
they'll be sent to *Jupiter Hall.*
Maybe it wouldn't be so bad
to send youngsters
out of their earth-bound bodies--
gift them with a moment
of astral flight.
Let them hang out on Ganymede
viewing cosmic storms.
Let them contra dance
on the rings of Saturn;
blow bubbles from the gilded
bathtubs of Venus.
I'd like them to experience a planet
that does not suffer
from lack of self-esteem.
Let these children
be born out of the head of Zeus
and rule over their own
gigantic selves.
Let them drink star light
through the straw of the Milky Way,
and graduate from the fishbowl
of time and space.
And blessed by the largess
of the universe,
let policemen unbuckle their gun belts
and float into the great orange eye
of Jupiter.
Where kids
are already kicking up
oceans of celestial dust.

The Emerald Café

I was sorry to hear
about the closing of the Emerald Café,
the place we met to read poems.
Understanding it had always been ephemeral—
a green vapor passing through
Dorothy's mind.
It's green glass steeples
standing in the middle distance,
in a near future composed of skipping.
Gleaming towers singing all things green—
because life is sweet.
The Emerald was too full of light
incapable of catering to
the lower appetites:
black and white hard scrabble,
dark tornados
and the cackle of scared pullets.
Maybe its owners miscalculated
the arc of rainbows,
the migration of blue birds
or the fact that Munchkins live on fat flowers
and refuse to sit at tables.
In any case, I'm sorry
to hear about the Emerald—
that the ghost of poems
will recede into its brick walls,
yellowing with time.
Already people forget the silk balloons
that brought them here from Omaha.
And the Wicked Witch
darkens the sky with doubts,
sickens the air
with rotten eggs of sulphur.
There is only one thing to do—
make the long journey back
to the Great and Powerful OZ,
and ask
what we always ask for in our poems:
a brain, a heart, some courage.

Vacuum

Today I vacuum the house
as if it had the floor plan
of the world.
I am ridding it
of all the contagions known to breed
in the larval magma of swamps
and the detritus that accumulates
in the gutters of forgotten streets.
I vacuum around
the foot of the sofa,
suck ancient dust from the boot of Italy,
maneuver carefully around the Cape
of Good Hope.
I sweep away the infections of Africa
and the scrofulous jails of America.
I give Mexico back its clean plazas
and restore luster to the tiara
of the Arctic Circle.
I lift Persian rugs
and suck hidden regimes
from the Middle East.
I vacuum the Atlantic's deep trenches,
liberate Polynesia's pristine palms
and uncover the rarified wood
of the rain forest.
I find dust bunnies
"down under," open the windows
of Albania and eradicate
cobwebs over the Balkans.
Finally I restore Tibet
to the top of a crystalline world.
There is no stopping my vacuum—
purifying the air
over charnel grounds and
democratizing colonial strongholds
by giving everyone a clean start.
Even monsters
at the edge of the world

change to butterflies
at the sound of my vacuum.
All the world's evils
spill into the "Whispertone" canister.
And the house becomes so light
it levitates,
spinning like a planet
in the immaculate corridors of space.
It glows liquid blue–
In the midst
of a white wedding of clouds,
like the cleanest corner
of the Mediterranean.
Just humming to itself
and waiting for an astronaut
to take its picture.
And in the background
(if you look closely enough)
you can just glimpse a touch
of chrome.

Alms Sandwich

This morning I prepare
peanut butter & jelly sandwiches
for the Redwood Valley monks.
As I spread the goo
I can't help but think of them
as young boys
with jelly mustaches.
How far they have come
over slags of evanescence and
through the long low tunnel
of desire–
past aisles of chrome
and gaudy tank tops
made in Bangladesh sweat shops.
And now for some reason
I remember the unkind step father
of my childhood
who sold fireworks and
plastic memorial wreathes
to freckle-faced kids and
widows leaning over cemetery mounds
like blemishes on the blank face
of western Kansas.
He tried to push me into sales
but I didn't have the stomach.
And so I passed through
the fluorescence of hungry markets
and the secondary light of mirrors,
searching for something
hidden in plain sight
like the arrowhead I discovered
at a baseball diamond
or the sutra embedded
in the box of a dull afternoon.
Somehow it all comes back
to these mongrel sandwiches
about to be transformed
through the hard currency

of the cells
into saffron clad bodies
that have taken refuge.
They walk their alms rounds
through the middle of town
and all I have to offer
is a glob of childhood
between a slice of birth &
a slice of death.
In return they offer a chant
which makes me feel so new
I can't remember
who is giving food
to whom.

San Francisco of the Spacious Mind

"... *flower nonetheless,*
with the form of the great yellow
Rose in your brain!"   ~ Allen Ginsberg

A friend placed a copy
of "Howl"
on the makeshift altar.
I hadn't realized Ginsberg died.
He seemed to go on forever
like that yellow flower
by the railroad tracks.
I thought of him
tough as a thistle.
Whitman's child.
Now he's entered smoke.
I'm not good at elegies
since I don't believe he's gone.
His eyes still squint
through coke bottle lenses
at a world crazy with pollen
and the disease of clinging.
Still the Poet of cherry bombs
under coffee cans;
genitals liberated from ice cube trays;
stars bursting over bed sheets;
junkie–needle–sirens–pricking–alley–bubble–nights.
Disembodied poet meditating on the Holy, Holy, Holy
fuzz of human kindness.

What would he have us write
about him?
That he is the ink
upon the page.
That he is the poem
coming into form.
That he finally mastered the long, yellowing line–
gone to seed out of exuberance.
That the pine trees will wear
their black berets at his funeral.

7

And that out of kindness
he will wear their needles
on his way to San Francisco
of the spacious mind.
I see the black and white
cover of "Howl"
on the altar.
Its big title
angry as a boil,
wild as the wet air
between lovers–
blowing down long train tracks
toward that great yellow flower.

Stars Over a Blue Field

Everyone is always trying to write
the great American novel–
what about the great American poem?
The one with the pair of steer horns
as a hood ornament.
The way the sky turns green
just before a tornado
over western Kansas.
The spontaneous combustion
of a ten day
used tire fire outside Akron.
The ghost of George Washington's
cherry tree.
Fifty stars
over a blue field.
Ferris wheels manufacturing
teenage electricity.
Alligators lurking the sewers
of Newark.
Smoke stacks, succotash, clapboards, crab cakes, Chevrolets,
Smokey Bear, bebop, fireworks, gospel choirs, antebellum spires,
french fries, dude ranches, one armed bandits, black-eyed-peas,
Barbie ensembles, pop-top cans, Window Rock, Tomorrow
Land...
The list could go on
beyond the manifest destiny of the moon.
The dawn's early light of swing sets.
The caffeinated anthem
of truck stops.
The transience of cottonwood seeds.
New Yorkers transplanted
to Santa Fe;
Santa Fe transplanted
to Bloomingdales.
Darkened letters in neon signs.
Frozen corsages
wrapped in cellophane.
Pennies flattened on railroad ties.

The way snow
appropriates the history
of prairies.
The religion of Wild Blue Yonder.
The fifty-first state of pressed flowers.
Walt Whitman singing the body electric,
Gene Kelly singin' in the rain.

Let the Nation Worry! *
(For the opening of a new wing of the Grace
Hudson Museum, Ukiah, California)

In 1926 the country jittered
like an electric arc
between two world wars.
And the Great Depression
began to stir in the dark closets
of over zealous bankers.
The whole country tilted
toward the engine of Gotham
under the weight of Prohibition,
while skyscrapers cut away
raw blue membranes of air.
Before the sky fell,
Grace Hudson mixed her oils
out West, under the totem of redwoods,
at the vanishing point of Pomo land.
In 1926 while lab-coated men invented
liquid-fueled rockets,
Grace Hudson
slowly painted the Pomo boy, Tsa-Kat,
accompanied by his dog.
The two are unconcerned
about Coolidge's Laissez Faire markets
as they stride out of the picture,
along the river.
Even the tip
of the delicate fishing pole
seems to quiver in excitement.
They say the face is hardest to capture.
And even though
Tsa-Kat is an orphan,
his face shines with something
beyond the painted sunlight.
In 1926, Grace labored long hours
amidst rumors of Pandora's
new industrialized Box
called "television."

And when she had
daubed the last bit of willow,
she wrote,
they play along the beautiful river
with no worries about 'lost lands'
or the 'coming generations.'
The sunshine of today is enough.
I believe her. I believe the immense difficulty
of catching this boy and his dog
mid-stride in happiness.
There will be time
to consider the cruelty of treaties
and the fate of future generations
too preoccupied with war and boarding schools
and abuse, to fish.
But for today,
let the nation worry!
Let Tsa-Kat and his dog,
lead us out of this world weariness
onto a path in the sunshine
where the beautiful river is enough.

*Title of a 1926 Grace Hudson painting

Why Walt Whitman was a Buddhist

*"...I do not talk of the beginning or the end... There will never
be any more perfection than there is now."*

Walt Whitman, *Song of Myself*

Before the formal photographs of the "Good Gray Poet,"
before you felt your bones at night
or dreamt uneasy dreams of young men buried
in fields of hard red wheat,
before the iconography of your curious smile
or the democracy of old age,
before the wild trailing vine of your song had gone to seed,
before you forded all the rivers,
typeset all the verses,
said goodbye to all the lovers,
before you posed for the aperture of posterity...
you practiced singing the body electric,
breathing the starry night,
watching a thousand, thousand geese
fill the sky with their beautiful words—
then pass away.
It was you singing to the night of sleepers
even in their graves.
Your emancipated slaves dancing in the firelight
next to overseers cutting heart shapes
out of Confederate flags.
Your libidinous, glittering, transcontinental mind
searching under every plantain for signs of life.
Wasn't it you that said, "the smallest sprout
shows there is really no death."
You, Walt Whitman, walking loose-limbed
into the field of each moment,
singing the Song of My Not-Self
from the pores of every peregrination.
You leaving Walt Whitman behind—
winging through the sheer effulgence of the New World,
watching it war with itself over tufts of cotton.
You who said, "Peace is always beautiful."
If you had seen the Buddha on a prairie road,

I feel certain you would have recognized him
and bowed down to receive his blessing.
And in that moment, you might have seen
your whole, seamless, unchanging, unalterable poem
abiding in the leaves of grass.

* Walt Whitman published his collection of poems, in various versions (ranging from twelve poems in 1855 to 383 in 1892), under the title "Leaves of Grass."

Vegetarianism

After a year
my son quit being a vegetarian
because he said it was too painful.
The craving for McDonald's hamburgers
was too strong.
It is the same urge
that compels him to step on ants.
And yet he is capable
of oceanic kindness.
How does a person approach
the two live wires of a paradox?
Can the devil who always wants
learn to share marbles
with the angel of sacrifice?
When does the mind
leave these two to work it out
in their sandbox?
There is a paradise
where the golden arches of fast food joints
stand by themselves,
where fear and fatigue evaporate
into the heaven of earth
and scars become stars
in a sky emptied of self.
It is the space between breaths
where new suns are born.
My son still refuses
to eat most kinds of meat
in deference to his stuffed animals.
He is immune from contradiction
because he still lives in a world
where everything speaks the same language.

Just Desserts

I was thinking about
the culinary arts class
that quit en masse,
and threatened to sue the school
because their instructor
refused to teach them *desserts*.
And that spiteful chef
seems to be everywhere at once—
lurking in the super market aisles,
behind me
snickering over recipes,
even in the kitchen
of my own chest.
He holds up a spatula
like the sword of Damocles
and forces us to learn the Latin names
of common vegetables.
He is the gym teacher
who made us pull down our shorts
to check our jock straps.
He is the small man
who always seems to wheedle
the DA or Bank Superintendent job
then lord it over any poor SOB
who looks at him cross-eyed .
In truth, he is a cream puff,
a Napoleon,
a pineapple upside down cake,
some devil's food.
I imagine his students
waiting around a corner
to pelt him with cream pies.
What makes a chef so surly?
Was he raised on castor oil
and sauerkraut?
Were Sunday Schools full of hellfire
and burnt bunt cake?
It's no wonder he stood

before his class
sharpening his paring knives
on their frustration.
Food can be a weapon
when it is withheld–
when it floats away
on clouds of meringue.
I am glad they rebelled–
threw off the yoke
of his arrogant Hollandaise,
sent him packing his mixing bowls.
This world is too full
of baked on grease and sorrow,
not to leave a little room for dessert.

Pencil

I am indebted to the yellow
number 2 pencil;
it is the bright line
between longing and
the lustrous carbon language
of the body.
It is the instigator of gray smoke
from wigwams
drawn in the wilderness
of Big Chief Tablets.
It is the genie of arabesque;
mother of doodles and
maypole of playful syllables.
It is a phone booth
crowded with freshmen vocabularies.
Its yellow molecules fill
with countless trembling verbs.
I've witnessed its ability
to erase history, to leave smudge marks
over misspelled sentiments,
to darken clouds with monologues of rain.
I've learned to release old nubs
to the place of dead pencils
where ghosts of unfinished poems
hover just above blue lines of college ruled paper.
I am fond of these ordinary
yellows rays quickening paragraphs
out of nothingness—
these honey hunters buzzing
pages of numinous clover.
The pencil is beautiful in its sunny simplicity,
a thing designed to make a point.
It has chosen the *number 2*
knowing that perfection is beyond
the notebook of this world.
It's name taken from the Latin for penis
by some Renaissance writer
with a sense of humor.

It fills a horizontal space
on the still life of a desktop,
but once vertical,
the whole blotter comes alive.
And if waggled just right
it performs the rubber pencil trick.
We can chew it,
beat it against Formica,
abuse it in a hundred ways—
and still it faithfully records
our secret marginalia.
It is the nascent portrait
on a cocktail napkin,
The gray filament
in the light bulb of our genius.
It is the shortest distance
between two points,
and the huge distances inside a nursery rhyme.
It is a slight weight
in the notch of the right ear,
poised like a canary.
This ordinary implement is a reminder
that even when we are dull
or hibernating in the locked drawer
of dark feelings,
we can flower ourselves
from the slender stem of sleep.
We can take this small, yellow stick
and make our mark on the earth.

The League of Slow Cities
"Good living is not only Italian–but it is very Italian."
~Mayor of Greve, Chianti (Tuscany)

Against the backdrop
of worried frescoes and
stunted cypress trees,
thirty Italian cities reclaim
plazas in the dark
where lovers stroll
around the central fountain
of their desire.
They band together
to rebuild the elongated tables
of El Greco
where extended families come to eat
and food is cooked as slowly
as a summer of green figs.
The League of Slow Cities
proclaim: this is our manifesto
and we stamp it with the logo
of a snail.
Now come, sit in the shade
of our Monuments To Ease;
nap in the somnolent coup
of the afternoon.
And empty the basket
of your dark moods
under the luscious, ripening
melon of the day-moon.
Remove the tight shoes
you were handed
on the first day of work
and cool your feet
in the slow riddle of the sea.
The League of Slow Cities
raises its brown hand
as if to say, please stay–
Must you hurry to be captured
in the neon light of fast food chains?

Disconnect your car alarms,
unburden yourself from the dead
weight of cell phones
and the fumigated kitchens of haste.
Place a sprig of rosemary
behind your ear and
taste this sausage
crafted from the body of a wild boar.
Gaze through the thick, green world
of olive oil;
take its Etruscan stock
onto the winter of your tongue.
And make it young.
Make it young!
The League of Slow Cities says
Enter the cathedral
of impossible ceilings rising up
to the God of slowed time.
Light a taper.
Lower yourself onto the dark wood
that shines from a thousand years
of sitting in prayer.
Toss the coins
of your hard, copper cares
into our fountains
and find the true origin of luck.
Retire governments of instant coffees.
Linger in the weather
of warm confessions;
taste the salty exaggerations
of new torsos
and sing *O Sole mio*
over a plate of chilled pears.

* Over 30 Italian towns have banded together to
embrace a slower pace that allows for enjoyment of
"the good life." Their logo is a snail inching past a
silhouette of modern buildings.

Instituto Fleming, Rome
([Ian] Fleming Intermediate School)

Pupils emerge
from the dark pool of puberty
in white tuxedos
wearing red carnations
like propellers.
Their dark hair
beautifully in place
atop every new encounter.
Their skin capable
of picking up a new language overnight.
The only junior high school
in the world
devoted to espionage–
Where students photograph
the top secret documents
of adulthood
with hidden cameras of instinct;
write notes with the invisible ink
of hormones.
They are taught to memorize
The food chain
and grin with the confidence
of Lord Byron.
They learn the applied arts of
ballroom dancing, skeet shooting,
scuba diving, judo and baccarat
as a means to an end
of the cold war of adolescence.
Children mature episodically,
licensed to kill with repartee.
Learn to escape every high window
by stringing one-liners together
like bed sheets.
In short,
a school that could only exist in Italy
with its mixture of olives and balconies,
basilicas and buffo.

Days that come
with the faint sound of applause
and nights that open
like old manuscripts
onto the 007 Hills of Rome.
A school of retractable desks
and windows composed
of martini glasses–
a school for the heart,
that prefers to be shaken
not stirred.

Ian Fleming is best known for his novels featuring British agent, James Bond (007), of Her Majesty's Secret Service. Instituto (Ian) Fleming is a private middle school in Rome— reputedly named after the author.

Santa Sabina Spring
(Santa Sabina Retreat Center)

It is spring at Santa Sabina.
The sainted sleep
down the centuries
under their Italian Cypresses.
Monastic birds
twitter a liturgy
to Sabina
in her long robe
of conifer.
It is spring
in my small cell
where nuns
carefully counted rosaries
like an abacus
of prayer.
Where the only sound
is the earth-bound voice
of ancient plumbing.
Still, I can almost hear
grape vines sprouting
under the wound
of Roman arches.
Santa Sabina
must have been canonized
for her immense silence,
for the soliloquy
of her gardens,
for the halo
of her rectitude—
for all the airy spaces
that hold the bones
of this old house.

Vishnu Comes for the Bees

A colony of Italian Honeybees
has lived in the southeast wall of the shed
for as long as I can remember–
feeding off the ivy and roses and oleander.
And now a beekeeper named Vishnu
comes to retrieve the hive
beneath old planks that have begun to pucker
under the summer sun.
The bees are so friendly
he needs no smoke
to induce their submission.
They let him gather
three pendulous combs
while they hum around his netted head.
Vishnu does not come to create or destroy,
but to preserve.
He arrives in thick clothes
under the mesh veil of the world
for the bees that work
to gather sunlight lodged in flowers.
As the middle deity,
he comes to preserve the sweetness of their labor.
Vishnu comes for the bees
that speak to the part of his brain
that buzzes with wonder.
He comes to collect them at midnight
when they cluster
around their remaining comb–
too cold to stir themselves in anger.
He simply scoops them into a bucket
as they cling to the sustenance of their history.
He means to mix them with his other hives
where they will institutionalize
the memory of old loose boards and ivy.
Goodbye *Apis mellifera ligustica*
Long may you thrive unmolested
on the subcontinent of your hive–
preserved in the perennial spring
of Vishnu's watchful eye.

While Watching the Mariposa Creek Rise

It has poured for forty days
and forty nights...
yet the downpour
is more like a scratchy soundtrack
than anything biblical.
It's easy to imagine Noah
standing on the flooded banks
of the old century
shaking his head.
But the rain simply rains
the way weather expands
to meet our expectations.
The rain is more like an excited crowd
waiting to hear Beethoven's Ninth,
or the big blue dog
of the mind
shaking itself off
before coming inside.
This storm contains all storms
past and future
and the nimbus of every spring
fringed in black.
Beethoven's choir of angels
trill their voices backstage
like rain.
The earth is saturated
with the well wishes
of distant relatives.
PG&E workers in yellow slickers
clear the roads
of weeping branches
so that fathers may reach the denouement
of home—
in a city of wet dogs
in a country of timpani
in a blue planet
in a universe forever raining,
amen.

Balloon Fish, Sea of Cortez
"They lead a very tragic life, ..."
    ~J.D. Salinger, *A Perfect Day for Bananafish*

On the first day
we find a perfect Balloonfish,
its fixed spines
puffed out in all directions
like death's pinata.
Scores of its deflated brethren
wash onto the altar of the sea—
spines flattened in obeisance,
graves marked by piles
of beach stones
and florets of white coral.
For days we search
for another just like it
so both boys
can bring one home.
We find the long musical scales
of a Cornetfish
and a whole Guitarfish
varnished in its brown skin,
the Byzantine dome of purple urchins
and oyster shells sunning
in their pearlescent sleep,
a pelican carcass empty of fish
and a frigate's hollow wing bones
waiting to rise above
the fetid runway of sand
the broken skeleton
of a Moray Eel
baring its indignant teeth
and a startled scorpion
skittering out of a rotting coconut,
metaphorical shells
of Purple Olives, Unicorns,
Apple Seeds, Coffee Beans, Sand Dollars
and Giant Keyholes.
We even come across

the skulls of cattle,
their long horns
pointing up toward
a heaven of lush grass.
There are feathers, fish skins and
ligaments of old sandals.
White-cap bones riffle
over an indigo sea.
And ghosts of cumulus clouds
drift over a sky of azul.
We pick our way
through the graveyard of Balloonfish
searching for a perfect unholy cactus
like the one we set aside
sharpening its enmity
under the desert sun.
We search and search
until we realize
that it is the only one
of all the placid, concave,
lifeless bellows of Balloonfish–
that died bloated
in a perfect state
of fear.

Miles in the Past
"[But] the stars that marked our starting fall away.
We must go deeper into greater pain,
For it is not permitted that we stay."—Dante, The Inferno

It's the middle of July
and I think I could
actually fry an egg on the sidewalk.
It's hot, but not hotter
than the hell we make
complaining about the weather
or imagining that the grass is always greener
on the other side of the fence,
even when there is no grass and no fence.
I think about my father
hobbling around on that swollen leg for weeks
until he found out it was broken
in two places.
Broken so badly the surgeon said
amputation was an option. That's hot.
Getting old burns like a magnifying glass
over last year's leaves.
I helped bathe my father
while he shifted his weight
to his good leg.
Dante didn't mention
that you can't ever avert your eyes—
even if you want to spare someone's privacy,
even if you're embarrassed.
There is no privacy in hell.
And the whole place stinks of embarrassment.
The only way to keep your eyeballs
from being singed
is to look straight ahead—
even if it's at your naked father
who used to listen to Miles
play *Kind of Blue*
in the darkened den
when everything was cool.

Butterfly World

The guides take pains
to remind us
not to touch them—
that if one lights on a shoulder,
consider it auspicious
like an angel whispering something
in your ear about gratitude.
But please don't touch them;
they are ephemeral,
composed of polka dots,
bits of mica and tracing paper.
They live on the nectar of flowers.
The guides say it's okay
To touch the petals all around us
which are only butterflies
mixed with a greater dose of gravity.
It's even permissible
to bump into one another
as we try to avoid
contaminating the satin scales
of their wings.
But please don't blunder
into the holy beings
that remind us
we will eventually emerge
from our cocoons.

Wen-siang *

Old poet Wen-siang
battling the sons of Ghengis Kahn
with the crescent of your verse.
Palpitating the mountain paths
for their wounds.
Your countrymen lie
in shallow graves beneath the Great Wall.
Your hair is white with exile.
Winter birds fly over
 your stationary hut.
Old poet meditating
on the shape of sorrow:
is it a bowl, a bell,
a burnt field, a body bleeding away?
Your homeland vibrates
with the sound of war horses.
Anxious wives wait
under the same moon
that seals your loneliness.
Poet Wen-siang
old age advances
like Mongol invaders,
yet you lean into the cushion of spring.
Farmers slave all day
to pay war taxes.
You have nothing to show
for your labors
except this thicket of poems–
you are free.

* Wen-siang was a Buddhist poet, and wayfarer who
 lived during the bloody thirteenth century Mongol
 invasion of China.

Sangha

My friend
traveled back to Wisconsin
to clean out

her mother's house.
She spent six weeks giving
things away

like a rope bed
to the historical museum.
She kept herself

moving up and down
through the memories
of her mother's home,

from basement to attic
and back again.
Every day chipping away

at the old stairs
until the basement sunk
into the good green ground

and the attic floated up
into Frank Lloyd Wright's
airy architecture

over Wisconsin.
It is springtide.
Her mother's moon wanes

inside the constellation
of her daughter's body.
Yet mother remains

in the scent of kitchens,
the glassine roses praying
in the afternoon sun,

the blue gaze
of the Midwest.
My friend talks about preparing

for the time
when her own children
will pack up her house.

Her eyes are bright.
She speaks as if shedding
a sleeve of opaque skin.

She comes back
to our circle
pink with release.

I listen, drifting in a kind of reverie,
the way the sky turns
just before it rains,

when suddenly
the person next to me
squashes a mosquito

against my bare knee.
In that moment
I realize

how important it is
to practice
dying.

Elegy for Pam

You chose the last
blue moon
of the century—
the one hovering
like the great blue bud
of spring.
So blue,
the tides break
like beat poems
whispering against the trillion
tiny pebbles of the body.
And now you lie still
in a blue dress
in the blue light
of death—
your hands
folded over your tummy
as an obeisance to birth—
the other side
of the color wheel.
And we sing
hallelujah
that you have been born
back into the buttery sweet
sun of peace—
where your hair grows
lush and blond
on the cancer-less beach
of all your good deeds.
Even as your body yellows
like the last burst
of maple leaves,
the ineffable hosanna
of things to come
begins to wrap itself
around you.
Around the choir

of your friends,
around the elegiac poppies
of your garden
and the corrugated road
leading to your home.
Around the Methodist steeple
down in town
and the sighing vineyards.
Around all the planets
of porch lights.
Around the wizened moon
whispering blue-petalled poems
to the starry egress
where Sufis dance
to a chorus of Allah.
Wrapping itself
all the way back
to the body on the bed
and the note card from Thoreau
that speaks for you
when it says: "I have an appointment
with Spring."

Crematorium

We slid you onto the conveyor
without ritual—
just three people
witnessing the heat
of your going,
our voices lost
in the blast furnace
between worlds.
Whatever I might have said
is just ashes.
I remember not knowing
what to do with my hands
as if they could speak
for me.
I remember the thoughtful attendant
with a knack
for disappearing into the drapery.
All of it as ordinary as small talk
with a bank teller—
as extraordinary as a constellation
in the shape
of the crematorium's cardboard box.
I don't know
what I'm trying to say
to you—
to the solar flames
that took you
into apprenticeship.
This poem is just my way
of listening to your echo,
so that I may
hold these spring days—
covered in their fine ash
of sunlight—
and say goodbye.

Walking Meditation

So much silence,
I can almost hear the song
of the pampas grass
on the bluff.
And I didn't realize
that the sun makes a sound
when it comes up
like an Indian squeeze-box,
only brighter.
I walk slowly, wordlessly
to a finger of the Pacific–
composed of that blue quiet
that allows fish
to sacrifice themselves
to one another.
Pain has a sound too.
It is the low dark hum
of the old generator
behind the barn of my childhood.
It insists on its place
next to the reminiscence of waves.
It deserves to carve out
its jagged space
in the sand–
otherwise how would I hear
the single clear note
of the sea bird's flight,
just now.

The Globe

As I pulled around the back
of the Goodwill store,
a globe rolled past me
as if the world were running away
from its orbit of old clothes
and the gravity of exhausted beds
or had decided to take pity
on Atlas' arthritic shoulders.
The globe of good will
shuttling past constellations of silverware
sending hemispheres swimming backwards
in their inebriated seas.
On this journeyman Monday,
the planet tried to quit
its complicated job.
But an employee chased it down
before it had a chance to roll
into the black hole of a ravine.
I felt a small sigh of relief
and some regret
that the world could never play hooky
like those who spin in contrary circles
over its flowered surface.
The dutiful employee carried the earth back
across the black expanse of asphalt
onto the loading dock.
And I thought about the world
rotating slowly on its cockeyed axis
under the porch light of the moon
always imagining that goodnight kiss,
but never stealing it.

Upon Finding a Discarded Santa Costume

At first I wasn't sure
so I circled around the block
to get a better look;
there it was lying on the trash heap
like someone who had fallen
or leapt from a rooftop.
The red coat
might have been soaked in blood.
It was unsettling–
not the great dislocation
of war or divorce,
but the kind that comes
with small losses of innocence.
Imagine a child
walking by wondering why
Santa threw away
a perfectly good pair of pants.
And what were they doing here
in the middle of summer anyway?
You can almost see him
screwing up his face
trying to puzzle it out.
And then the awful recognition.
Maybe it's just me,
but I feel sorry
for the imaginary child
and his very real loss.
Couldn't the perpetrator
just put the costume
in a black garbage bag?
Or better yet, burn it
and watch the ashes
make their long trip north.
Or even better,
wait until the creatures stop stirring
then leave it neatly laundered
next to the plate
that holds a sugared cookie or two.

A Bad Case of Chicken Pox...

clutter his face, punctuate
his jawline, dot
his skull with a stand
Of nettle. Vesicles erupt
like volcanoes under his innocent
prehistoric arms.
At night he rises in the steam
of bad dreams—sleep walking through
a mine field of scabs
embossed with red
serial numbers.
His body: a child's
salt & flour map of some foreign
mountain range. I try to
catch a glimpse of him holding
still behind all those bumps,
like a wounded deer.
The tender shadow behind his ears,
enduring the aftermath of a hornet's nest.
His open face
presaging the pimpled lacunae of adolescence.
A dark crop of curls
hangs over a line of barbed wire.
He tucks himself
Into a ball
where the other kids
can't see him.
I have to roll my sleeves up and
reach way down to feel the full length
of his untroubled brow.
They have even popped out
on the roof of his mouth—
his whole body threatens to catch
fire. Thank God
just now I hear the gentle
splash of rain against the house.

Exchange Student

Teenage girls converge
on a dark Israeli exchange student
standing at the 4 foot line.
He speaks the seamless Esperanto
of sun and sinew—
brings a Mediterranean glow
to the middle of the pool.
The girls step into the myth
of the shining body,
place their eager arms around the exotic boy
up to his chest in blue water.
They laugh and splash
in easy combinations—
drawn to the slim waist
of his guileless presence.
He is the statue of their ideal lover,
the best of what is to come
out of the hallways of high-school
and beyond.
He is a boy of desert heat
come to initiate them
into the sacredness of water.
And for his part, he is lost in play—
translating their gestures
with his whole body—
leaping like a dolphin
before the churning tourist boat
of their desire.
In a few weeks he will be called back
as a conscript to his homeland.
In the blink of an eye,
the girls will graduate from
the swimming pool.
And he will stand in his army fatigues
shading his eyes against the desert sun.
And it will all seem like a mirage.

Two Poems From the Police Blotter

1. Bear Accident

Seven days before the solstice
when bears should be floating
in the emulsion of sleep
and dark roads should be ribbons
on boxes of silence,
an 18-wheeler hit a large brown bear
near the Hog Farm Commune
north of Laytonville.
The truck veered off the road
and struck a tree.
The bear was dragged,
the driver ejected
and buried by the truck's cargo
of frozen fish.
The driver suffered a broken arm.
But what was the bear
doing in the middle of the road?
Was it ruminating
on the broken white lines
as if they were schools
of inaccessible fish?
Did it believe
in the omnipotence of bear—
that nothing could drag it
over the edge of itself
into a black hole
ritually dug by commune members?
The bear should have been buried
in frozen fish.
Eternity should have looked like
clean fish bones
instead of dark stars of dirt.

2. Tuperware Assault

We think we can contain
the danger sharpening itself
in the pockets of our discontent,
that our lips can hold in
words that live on broken glass.
That we can hypnotize
our fingers from making the sign
of the plucked bird.
We tell our hands
to imagine they are emerging from cocoons
or that they should only be used defensively
like umbrellas or sparingly like
alarm clocks. We make our hands
into a steeple and teach them
to love horizons. We teach them
to follow the fingerprints of Victorian gardens.
We teach them to read.
They ripen at our sides
like clusters of handsome fruit—
stay close like pilot fish.
They paint pastorals and
learn to tame steering wheels.
We tell ourselves
that we will remain inside the air tight
hospitality of morning
even in the face of militant neighbors
and the injuries of jury duty.
We tell ourselves that we will be spared;
that we will spare the clumsy
dime store clerk, that we will keep
our hands occupied with cradles of yarn—
keep a lid on the miniature volcanoes
of our parent's unblessing.
But not so today
for the man who struck his girl friend
with the nearest thing at hand,
a plastic container of leftovers—
taking cold nourishment
from the dying animal of her trust.

Seven Thousand Miles West of Troy

The taxi stops
at the cycloptic eye
of the traffic light.
On the left,
the *Iliad Book Shop*
stands shoulder to shoulder
with the *Odyssey Video Store*.
What would Homer think?
A thousand ships
tucked neatly under
Helen's technicolor sleep.
A simple stroll
down the block
under the rosy-fingered
exhaust of Vineland Street.
Achilles falls
on the strip mall–
The war
of the market place
is always
one part ocean &
nine parts salt.
Odysseus stranded
on the island
of a video cassette,
while Penelope patiently
weaves the sexual homecoming
we call the past.
The tongue thickens
around Ithaka,
as if the waves themselves
might congeal
into sidewalks
of some monstrous
metropolitan spell.
And the boulevards fill
with wooden horses
in the shape of automobiles.

We wait for pedestrians
in the narrow crosswalk
of their mortal wounds
to drink the water
of forgetting
that we call LA.
And as the light turns green,
we catch just a glimmer
of Elysian Fields.

Fly

A fly bangs against the window
wounding the short time
it has left on earth.
Its sky has hardened into glass.
The fly rests on the sill
deciding what runes to scroll
on the pane.
It cuts across the room,
slams back into the window
which looks out
over the Black Mission Fig.
The world is much softer
on the other side
where late afternoon sun
dapples the heavy-lidded grass.
It seems that the fly has given up,
but it simply regroups
within its multitude of eyes.
The fly buzzes to itself,
making incantations with its wings.
It is trying to find the space
between molecules of silica
so that it may go
where the air is not trapped
in silence.

Prairie

I never finished the 622 pages
of the book about the prairie
because I never finished the prairie.
I left right after the high school of Kansas
on page 239—
when grasses turn
the color of overdue library books.
Though I lived on the state line,
(with its intimation of hills)
traveling west required a long push
past the blowzy manifesto of prairie.
It stood like a storm
of evangelical murmurings
each testifying
in its own unvarnished pew.
Mostly I couldn't tell
where earth met sky
like the flat dialect of pennies or
the closed screen doors
of destitute farmers.
I left because the prairie lends itself
to the far sighted or the crop duster
or the monk.
But not the young,
not the ones still flowering
In their differences.
I left without leaving a dent
In the grass
or the lugubrious weather.
I am convinced that nobody
ever finishes the prairie;
It finishes you.
Even the author
of the ambitious book,
lost his sense of climax—
he just went on
searching for adjectives.

I can't blame him
for trying to make a prayer
out of the irascible prairie grass,
or for pitting numinous language
against the numerous landscape.
I don't know who won—
I didn't finish— but I can guess.

Cowboy

The guy ordering a hamburger
wears a "Cowboys for Christ" tee-shirt
that says, *I pony up for Jesus.*
It makes me sad
that cowboys trade in their sunsets
for eponymous tee-shirts
branded in the
tight corral of religion.
If he could just stop
to consider the miracle
of roasted coffee,
small tables varnished in candlelight
and the big girl with a pony tail
who takes his order
with such solicitousness—
he might throw off
his tee-shirt right here and now,
like Assisi tossing away
his father's riches.
He might gather
horses and cattle around him
and compose a prayer
to innocence
that would protect them all
from slaughterhouse and
glue factory.
He might feel so strongly,
in this moment,
that all the impious tee-shirts
within ten blocks,
would turn back
into soft tufts of cotton.

Following a Truck in Foul Weather

I followed
as the driver
of *the Cow Chow* truck
down shifted
through melancholy towns
suckling at the great udder
of Clear Lake.
Followed in the big rig's wake
as it churned the grass
of the highway into milk
splattering my windshield.
I didn't care much.
He was just doing his job—
sluicing through the black & white
holstein drops of rain.
I watched the way
other truckers
blew their horns
and flashed their lights
in solidarity,
the way one might
lower one's heavy body
in the shade next to another,
to watch beleaguered travelers
rush by.
Every so often
I'd catch a highway sign
marking the distance
with white letters
on a green background—
like a false spring.
Then back to the blue pasture
of lake
receiving its cold seeds of rain
and the behind-end of truck
with its bumper sticker:
"Without trucks, America would stop."

And I thought,
Why not stop?
We could all graze together—
explore the ways we devour
the world
through our four stomachs.
Breathe a bovine mist
over trailers
darkening the lakeside hamlets.
We could bellow
over the sweet grass
of our amplitude
until a whole lake
of foul weather and diesel fumes stopped,
then disappeared.

Godzilla (On the 50th Anniversary of Hiroshima)

The two boys on the couch
simply don't understand
that Godzilla has already eaten
the heart out of Japan.
That he is, in a word,
real.
Standing 400 feet above the past.
And that some try to read the future
in his footprints.
He has already turned cities
into grainy black and white miniatures.
Places swallowed up
by ordinary people running over the edge
of the world.
The two wide-eyed boys
feel sorry for him.
They think the cities are just too small
and cramped—
made of popsicle sticks.
He can't help stepping on passenger trains.
They just don't understand
that our psyche is shaped
like the archipelago of Japan.
And that this monster
has been unleashed there.
They watch him finally killed
by an "oxygen destroying" bomb
corroded until only his spiky bones are left drifting
through the murky water of Tokyo Harbor.
They simply don't understand
that Godzilla still resides
in the depths of his own dark marrow.
His oxygen-depleted eyes
peer out from the blue light
of the television.
Not ten feet
from where the boys sit
against a pattern of white flowers.

Homeless

"O tender and wondrous thoughts,
Of life and death, of home and the past and loved,
and of those that are far away."
　　~Walt Whitman, *By the Bivouac's Fitful Flame*

When I am sick at heart
and tired of the indentation
I call home,
in a world that has lost its orbit–
I think about old Father Whitman
in a loose muslin shirt
ministering to amputees
under the oilcloth of a Union tent.
He chose to make his way
through the waist-high prayer of prairies
before the world slipped the circle
of its gravity.
And now I feel his shadow
fall across the unreconstructed South
of hard longing.
At these times,
it seems we have each sacrificed
a limb to slavery
and to the great cause of its unmaking.
Whitman was a patriot.
He made a home out of usefulness,
mopped the brow of scared recruits
and made a soft place
in their suffering. A home of sorts,
for the wailing wounded men
who missed their mothers,
their sweet hearts, their brothers—
waiting dispossessed inside distant windows.
When I am sick at heart
and dizzy from tracking
the soul's wobbly circles of deprivation,
I think about St. Whitman
smoothing down the cot sheets
for some homeless son

under the cold light of Confederate stars.
He lights a lamp,
looks upon their ravaged faces,
tells himself this is a Civil War
between warring angels–
then cuts another row of bandages.

Santa Maria

on a good day
we realize
how things never really

drop off the edge
of the world
how a world flattened

by departures
does not end
in the jaws of sea serpents

but returns to itself
round as an empty bowl
holding the sacred

bones of our creations
how ships also arrive
on sunlit beaches

how the Santa Maria
must have discovered
the roundness of the world

as gratitude
on a good day
we realize how many

people pass through
our bodies
on their way home

Emptying My Parent's Liquor

We gather up the bottles:
sweet vermouth sipped after the ballet;
gin with its hint of juniper
to soften the cigarettes;
pina colada mix
poured over islands of inhibition;
miniature whisky pocketed from an airline;
cream sherry waiting for its Stroganoff.

My bother and I take turns
emptying the clear, amber, red, watery, viscous, fruity, acrid,
bitter surfeit
into the stainless steel sink.
Grenadine from the syrupy sixties.
Dinner wine still holding sunlight
from forgotten vines.
And scotch at the golden end of long days.

One by one we release the ghosts
of cocktail parties
and genies of extra dry gimlets.

My parents used to light up the *Manhattan*
of one another's skyline,
ask *Tom Collins* to join their conversation,
walk home under the constellations
of a pinot noir.
Now they rest their tired feet
on small ottoman's of utter sobriety.

The overstated, legendary, dark-grained, massive, sophisticated,
implacable
liquor cabinet was the only piece of furniture
my father kept after the divorce.
Now it gathers the dead air
of a museum piece.

I remember Madam Butterfly
turned up loud enough
to bend the backyard flowers
and strawberry daiquiris
where my parents floated
sunny and naked on pink ice.

And now we empty it all.
Goodbye vodka; goodbye maya; goodbye purple veils
between the earth of our undertaking and that other earth of
luminous boulevards;
goodbye hangovers; goodbye paper umbrellas you could almost
snatch from the air.

Sylvia Plath's Bees

I think about Sylvia Plath's bees—
each in its little jacket,
heavy with sweetness and guarding
its single momentous sting.
I can see their black bodies
buzzing against her yellow flowers,
gathering the sexual residue
which keeps them humming
through the afternoon of their short lives.
Every now and then one stings her
and she registers what it's like
to give up her life—
how its pain so easily passes
from this world of damp roses.
The meadow bends in obeisance
while the queen dreams of narcissus
and delivers her brood
into six sides of sweetness.
I am thinking of the economy
of Sylvia Plath's bees,
how precisely they shape the darkness
with the confessions of flowers,
how they punctuate the hedgerows.
I think about Sylvia Plath
watching her bees pack all that sweetness
in their dark wooden boxes.
She is young and in her prime
marveling at the strange, lovely bees
without whom the world would come
to a dead stop.
They are so drunk with work
that they don't notice her
watching their enormous landings.
She hovers like a god
beginning to swell in spots
where they've touched her with their blessings.

Skunks

It wasn't the gray wolves or grizzly,
badgers, bobcats, marmots
or even the otter lolling on its back
in the foam and mucilaginous seaweed,
but the family of skunks
so intent on the hunt
and unaware that they were already dead.
The young one hung back between its parents
as they headed out of their dusty diorama—
perhaps toward the diaspora
of some human community–
their black glass eyes alert,
their monumental odor barely contained
within the membrane of their vigilance.
I imagined them at dusk—
their white stripes
rippling like a false surrender
in the direction of the reposing fox.
It wasn't even the half exposed weasel
dragging its dead mouse
into the depths of its dead den,
or the antelope cutting the musty air
with antlers accustomed to the hermetics of bone.
It was these three skunks
stitched into a silence deeper than new snow,
alone in the world,
emphatic that–no matter what the variegated fawn
or camouflaged prairie dogs said—
life and death were black and white.
The skunk family accepted the poses
of despondent taxidermists,
surrendered to a world
frozen in predation and dried flowers,
adjusted to the metaphysical properties of glass.
And they gazed out with something like compassion
on tourists who shimmered like dust motes
in the filtered light
of the natural history museum.

Eulogy For Elaine
(May 15, 1930 - January 24, 2002)

I lie in the bed
where my stepmother lay
so many painful hours trying to make sense
of the ceiling's virgin snow—
unblessed with a prescience
of what the day would hold
in the tight bud of its stubborn fist.
I lie in the belly of the great blue whale of twilight
inspecting the enormous ribcage
of a private life.
The curtains are drawn and the room swells
against the four walls of the past.
I imagine her before the war
lying on a bed of Illinois clover
surrounded by the innocence of animals
and a wind break of domesticated trees.
I watch her stretch the girl-muscles
of her non-varicose legs.
I watch her hum the anthem of the future
down the dusty sidewalks of Albuquerque....
Could she have imagined this life
now drying on a clothesline between the stars?
Did she allow someone to comfort her
at the end?
We loved each other by loving the same family—
an oblique, moon-tinted affection,
but love nonetheless.
She would have liked what everyone said
at the ceremony,
though she'd probably busy herself in the kitchen.
I have joined a whole planet of bereaved
wondering, like my brethren,
why we don't say these things to the living.
It's time to say good-bye,
but I linger in her bed
staring up, searching for her
now that the ceiling has vanished.

Tristan and Isolde

While Tristan and Isolde betray their king
an unmistakable cough
escapes from the background.
It clings to the thin air of the balcony
even as the Prelude's notes fail
into the velvet of the concert hall.
The cough– on an otherwise pristine recording–
gives even Wagner a human touch.
It sends ripples out over the staid Swiss listeners.
It is a cough of liberation and imperfection
that belongs to the percussion section.
The small interruptions
remind us of the catarrh that does not yield
to the swelling strings of our astral bodies.
There it is again.
The spasm begins to punctuate the music
like a metronome with a loose spring–
a syncopation that sends the saints
of the orchestra pit out to scour the audience.
We all know what it's like
to sit with a tickle in the throat,
sandwiched between strangers;
it is how we spend our days.
The music speaks to love and death,
but the cougher must be absorbed in embarrassment–
a small, acute emotion
that can only look up to the larger passions
like a child to its parents hoping for a pat on the head.
I have lost track of the music,
waiting for the next expectoration–
like a single bird winging through a vast sky.
I would like to tell the inflicted
to go home and drink chamomile tea,
but this recording was made years ago.
And he or she has probably forgotten
that night in Zurich
when Wagner's deep purple veils
were rent by an ordinary cough.

For the Love of Music

When the doorbell rings,
it's usually a stranger,
often a salesman— rarely
a friend. A friend knocks.
This time it was a boy with crooked
glasses and peach fuzz.
He carried a clipboard,
readied himself (for the twentieth time)
to make his pitch— framed inside
someone else's porch.
When I opened the door,
he looked up like a deer caught
in the act of eating
my roses: fearful and
perplexed. He began—his beginning
filled with half-spent words,
starting and stuttering, falling and
and dusting himself off,
forcing fat words out through
the narrow adjustments of his
mouth. I did not interrupt,
though I wanted to.
I admired the courage to utter
his staccato script about piccolos
and yellow bus rides into the gloaming
of other high school auditoriums.
He was moving along the arpeggio
of the street raising money for the band,
forcing his words to order
themselves inside the small porches
of strangers. It took
a long time to sift through
the dissonance of his appeal.
By the time it was over,
I wanted to help pluck
thorns from his injured speech.
Instead I handed him five dollars.

Setting out to Write a Poem About the Birth of Jazz

The narrator said they played everything
New Orleans audiences could want:
waltzes, mazurkas, schottisches, polkas, rags, spirituals,
blues—performed all over town
at street parades, funerals, tea dances, picnic grounds
and balloon ascensions.
It was the image of a giant hot air balloon
rising slowly over
the narrow dance halls of Storyville,
counterpoising its bright billows
against the sinking cemeteries
of discolored churches—
that made me stop.
I could make everything else fit my world—
stretch it, slow it down,
open quaint spaces
for tailgate trombones and cornets
carrying the dearly departed
over Basin Street's rococo railings,
past the old man
on the dark side of the moon
playing the blues,
on to a heaven of big pearly pianos
and gospel swoons,
but I could not improvise balloon ascensions.
I could see balloons
rising in the background
of certain oil paintings,
but I could not place myself
under their shadows.
I could find the blowsy balloon fields
by the Mississippi,
but by the time I'd arrive—
the balloons would be long gone,
blown over the rainbow
by world wars, psychoanalysis
and the invention of x-rays.
I could see the whole tableau—

but the balloons were too lovely
and too light,
too much of the earth
before it became preoccupied—
too much of that easy other earth.
They were filled with too much heat and mystery
as they rose into the brilliant
tan and black and brass polyphony
and disappeared.

Dishwasher

I remember a dwarf
who stood on a step stool
counting and bundling silverware
for an endless line of Kansans
loading their trays
with cool squares of Jell-O.
And the black head dishwasher
who hated pimply-faced kids
from the suburbs—
barking his orders like a despot
among the gravy-smeared dishes
and disfigured slices of banana cream pie.
This was my first job—
steam cleaning platters of over fed desire
in the heartland,
near the stockyard,
under the saucer of a Kansas moon
and the table settings of stars
neatly bundled by some demi-god.
I worked under the pink eye
of the Putsch's Cafeteria highway sign.
Scoured acres of meat and potatoes
in the cafeteria of Kansas–
for love
of a sixteen year old bus girl.
Every night I was filled up
like the glass salt shakers
at the end of a shift.
I remember how the black drill sergeant
dipped his flask at closing time,
how women in white uniforms
waited for a city bus
into the hungry mouth of Kansas.
And I remember how the stars
over Putsch's parking lot
seemed dwarfed by our love.

Putnam Hall

I stand barefoot
four floors above
the Chippewa River
watching it change.
This ocher linoleum
has seen its share of ashes,
scuffs, sperm dollops, sebum and spittle.
I imagine the young man
who came here last semester
already sloughing off
the epidermis of high school.
Standing in this spot
he must have looked out
over the Chippewa
and shivered.
I rise from the lower bunk
amidst dust motes and
halos of farm girls
deflowered in the recesses
of Putnam Hall–
sensing their ephemeral weight
in the bunk above me.
I can almost hear roommates
recount the nights
they sparked like fireflies
until their bodies
burned themselves out–
the river below
catching their unfiltered cigarettes,
and ashes
one by one
like flakes of snow.
Still, I imagine a morning
when this young man
became holy
falling into a moment of river.
Though it was already passing.

Up Here

Up here
we have become
something like fish
dropped into an aquarium.
In our pressurized cabin
we can not hear each other's body
reconciling to the air.
We have adopted the death-mask
of fish:
fossilized flowers drifting
over the blue equivalent of Texas.
Unlike fish,
we will return to our element
where junkyards look like junkyards
instead of aerial mosaics,
and rivers are burdened with old tires
instead of light.
We will return to the cracks
of our lives
that appear seamless from up here.
We will return to redeem
small pieces of sidewalk
that threaten to break off
and float away
and farms that fervently believe
in the same orderliness as sky
but fail back into the earth.
The man across the aisle
wants to chat;
he does not realize
he has become a fish,
a bird, a flower—
that words are stillborn
up here.
He doesn't realize
he's left his old life.
He doesn't realize
how powerful this plane must be

to rise above our regrets.
Above those we kiss goodbye
as if screwing the lid
back on a jar.
And though we wrap ourselves
in hope,
it seems as distant,
as the patchwork of East Texas–
from up here.

911

A poet said it's too big
to get your arms around.
And I think he's right,
the pit is too close
and too vast.
So I'll say it obliquely—
not like that jet
flying straight into the building;
not like the gash in the skyline
or the bone white ash.
It seems everyone
knows someone or knows someone
who knows someone
who was in one of the buildings.
We have so few words
large enough to approach sorrow,
it's a wonder
anything grows amidst the rubble.
Another writer said
it is so big and deep
we will all be working it out
in our dreams–
like the smoke that still lingers;
like the photographs on a makeshift memorial wall
in the Lower Manhattan
of our collective unconscious.
I am glad Jung missed this tragedy.
I am glad both sets of grandparents
missed it too.
They went to their graves
believing the new world was safe–
bless their souls.
It should be addressed gently
through small, everyday things:
birds flying south,
a pink cloud,
a cup of oolong tea–
The quiet things that hold

only an ounce of sorrow.
After all, how can we
grasp these waves of shock,
and after shocks—
the sickening call
for dental records,
the dull mountain
of charred picture frames.
Like the poet said,
it is too big to hold
except in silhouettes
and shadows.

The Last Two Members

They stand at opposing ends
of the Kabul synagogue
lighting Hanukkah candles
in the darkness of the temple ruins.
They are the last of thousands
who enjoyed latkes,
played dreidel deep into the Afghan night.
The old one throws a bent shadow
against a bare wall.
The younger man lights his candles
on a window sill.
They both prayed
for the end of the Taliban
and now they rejoice
at opposite ends of their unholy feud.
The old one, the synagogue caretaker, says,
"For a thousand and thousand years
our forefathers have celebrated these nights,
and now Jews all over the world
are celebrating too.
But with him it is not possible.
He is a bad person—
I am afraid of him."
The younger one, simply:
"That man is my enemy."
They accuse one another of everything
from running a brothel
to stealing sacred objects.
And in the ruined temple of their trust,
they have given the Torah to the Taliban
for safekeeping.
Now the Taliban and the Torah are gone.
And they are the last.
So tonight, across a broken courtyard,
they light tapers
celebrating the victory
of a small band of Jews
and the cleansing of the Temple.

But there is no brotherhood
to build a synagogue between them
and not even the half light of irony
to brighten their solemn prayers.
These two, these last members
of the congregation of Kabul,
turn their backs to one another
and speak into the drafts:
Blessed art thou O Lord, our God
King of the universe,
Who has sanctified this moment
And commanded us to kindle
The Hanukkah lights.

*Adapted from an Associated Press article by Laurie King,
December 10, 2001.

When I lived in Greece
"I do not speak of the past, I speak of love"
"The Thrush," George Seferis

Poems mattered.
People stapled them to bulletin boards
and not just in the communist districts.
They appeared alongside handbills,
inside apartment elevators,
wallpapered to construction sites
and smeared under cold columns of rain.
The acropolis stood in the moonlight
like a beautiful broken rhyme.
Students argued over poems
and held them naked
under the noses
of sublimated widows dressed in black.
Byron's ghost sang for reinforcements;
dolphins sprung their delicate rhythms
and the sea applauded loudly
against the pebbles of history.
Poems were eaten like pomegranates—
crept up the walls like purple bougainvillea.
Poems liberated statues,
sweetened the sheep's grass of ravaged islands.
Poems pooled in tavernas like ouzo—
like mercury running together into long demotic lines,
punctuated only by men playing cards
on the three-legged table of afternoon.
Poems mattered;
they threw shadows across the junta—
pulsated like pink scars incised in marble.
Poems were found plastered
to the sides of buildings no longer there.
Poems mattered to those
who endured the loss of loved ones,
sat in the sun shucking green almonds—
confident there would always be more.

Notes to an Italian Cypress

I always thought I'd end up
in your narrow shade
writing poems to honey-colored statues
ready to come to life;
that in the narcissism of my full stomach
I could will them into life
under your cool glance.
I never figured myself for a government job
and a ranch style house;
I never guessed I'd invest in orthodontia
and plastic wading pools.
I always saw the Mediterranean
laid out before me like a wet canvas
and little white washed churches
waiting for the simple bell of my sleep.
I could almost feel myself
clutching a wine glass at twilight
waiting for the first star
and the next and the next and the next
until everything was soaked in light
and me bathed in cosmic arousal.
I didn't figure on ministering the dog's heartworm pills.
I just didn't realize my hair would disappear
in the pattern of a monk's tonsure
or that exotic women would notice me
only as a reflection in a window.
I saw myself leaning against your body
happy for your eternal shade—
always young, always proselytizing to marble figures
about the religion of the flesh
when it emerges from the sea.
I made you into pillars of my imagination
so that I could prop myself
against your straight, unequivocal rising.
Even now, I don't need to close my eyes
to see you on some distant summer hill
shading a depression in the grass
where I once sat.

Dracula Park

A few miles outside Casa Vlad Dracula
in the forest where wolves still lurk
among the fir trees,
a German consortium prepares to break
ground for Dracula Park.
Besides the rides, restaurant
and arcades, they plan
an international center of vampirology.
The whole enterprise
a monument to Vlad the Impaler,
the Transylvania Count
with the long memory
and manic appetite for death.
Bram Stoker must be rolling
slowly over in his grave
as the wind carries rumors from Romania
about a Dracula golf course
and horseback riding
for pasty English tourists
who wrap themselves in heavy mufflers.
I have nothing against improving
Sighisoara's roads, electricity, waterworks...
I'm all in favor of renovating
the pastel walls of the old fortress town.
It's just all those bats
dislodged from their milky sleep—
cheapening themselves into souvenirs
and lamb-white clouds
injected with the black ink of accountants
to look heavy and threatening
over the phony mud of a Gothic castle.
And what about Vlad's 100,000 victims?
Will their ghosts be forced to ride
the miniature train encircling Dracula Park?
I imagine there will be rats, lots of them—
chocolate rats, rat tokens, rat jackknives
rat candles, bookends, pendants, postcards, nightlights,
rats streaming out of every kiosk.

Isn't it enough
that we expose our tender throats
at every dark opportunity?
That we nearly throw ourselves
onto the sharp vagaries of this life?
Must we buy tickets to be reminded
of the long fingernails
that clutch us from behind?
What good can it possibly do
to look into the night sky
suddenly burdened with teeth?
Or worse, to look into the sunlight
and know we are doomed?

Empty Pet Store

An empty pet store
is a sad thing
on a Saturday night,
when you're driving around
after fighting with your wife.
You expect exotic birds
to sleep
with their day-glow heads
tucked neatly beneath a wing
or iguanas to bury their green snouts
in Polynesian moons
of guava fruit.
You think maybe you'll catch
a glimpse of fluorescent light
from the aquarium tanks
of Siamese fighting fish,
or the granular glow
of a yellow bulb suspended
over baby Easter chicks.
She said that I couldn't do anything right,
that I was inadequate,
that as a husband, I sucked.
Things an animal would never understand.
Yet I go to work every morning,
love my young,
hang up my clothes—
everything an animal might do
if he were me.
Her disappointment must be something
higher up on Maslow's hierarchy;
something on Darwin's most elite list.
It's a sad thing—
this great dark corner
where the parrot, "Captain,"
stood on his low perch
mimicking customers,
where tarantulas pretended
to be big brown flowers

waiting for a nursery van
and crickets—bred as food–
strummed their ukuleles
under the bright green EXIT sign.
I sit at the traffic light
that turns red
in recognition of the loss
and imagine box turtles
conducting slow marches
under their lacquered band shells
and the king snake
coiling around the bones
of a rodent's hard luck.
The pet shop,
without its aura of feathers,
looks like any other vacant building.
And I stare at the red hand
over the cross walk
that says there is nothing left to pet.

For My Brother, Steve, on his 50th Birthday

I have not been trained to write a poem
for my brother.
I might as well pretend
that I store the North Star's light
or that I have never been caught
day dreaming.
I remember lush moments
growing up in the shade
of my brother's experience. As if
I would always be a year and a half
behind. Perhaps I was.
This is what I'm talking about.
I can't quite remember
who tattled on whom,
whose sexual adventures
merited more column inches,
whose losses accrued more gravity.
It seems to me
he stayed up late studying chemistry
while I tried to read
the physiognomy of the moon.
This is also what I'm talking about—
I can only really remember
searching that hypnotic lunar face
for something of myself.
Poems will turn themselves
inside out
trying to become bodies
of reflected light.
Sometimes it's hard to differentiate
my brother from myself,
so maybe there is still a chance
of saying something
that won't blow away.
It is hard to speak
about a brother's love–
easier to ask why birds sing
or why the ocean refuses

to exchange its salt
for something less dispersed.
It's all huge and complicated
by manuscripts of memory
and every day events
that paper over
the enchantments of brotherhood.
This is what I'm talking about.
I should have stopped at the North Star.
But I never learned how.

Giving Back the Green Sand
" ... the beach is composed chiefly of peridot,
a semiprecious gemstone. "

I realize now
that this vacation is about
giving back the green sand
my son took unawares
from the emerald outline
at South Point.
He did not understand
about Pele
and her green fire.
He just wanted something special
to share with his best friend
back home.
So the sand sits drying
in a tin pan;
it flickers begrudgingly
like fire from dark coal.
I ask him to consider
not taking something
that belongs to the island.
Giving back is so hard.
He crosses his arms and looks stormy
like one of the carved Tiki Gods
sold in Kailua.
I can see in his dark green eyes
he understands that the sand
has its own rules–
and that returning is one of them.
But he is stubborn
like his parents
who often withhold grains of affection
out of ignorance.
Still, we ask him to look
into the little cove of his heart,
to feel the magnet
of yellow sun and blue sea
and the goodness of their beach-green admixture.

But I do not know what will happen.
Granules of green light
sift through the hourglass
of his deliberations.
We strain to hear the ocean
inside the shell of his hard resolve.
He is new to this beach
composed of tiny rough choices–
just starting to make his pact
with the earth.
But he is still very green.

Midnight In The Emergency Room

My son has already grown used
to cradling his arm
as if he were holding some
orphaned animal out of the dark
and angulated cold.
His x-rays shine
on the screen behind us
showing a new tributary
in the moonlit river of bone
flowing down his small, sleeveless arm.
The emergency room is awash
with fluorescence.
My son is scared.
I keep looking back at the x-rays
expecting his fragmented bones to merge.
It is almost the magic hour
of midnight
and we are able to see
clean through one another.
Soon my son starts to slip
into the marsh light of morphine.
The doctor asks him
how old he is.
He says five.
A few moments later
he has grown so luminous
that when asked again,
my son says he is zero
and falls asleep.
His eyelids flutter from the effort
of carrying his arm
o deep in his body.
He cries out once
when the bone is set.
And when he wakes
his arm holds itself—
flows together
like the two bones of a clock
at midnight.

What Goes Up
(for Ana)

Every split second
a cell drifts
past the western shores
of the body–
mixes with the damp exhalations
of honey bees.
All things turn themselves over
as if they were soil,
their earth as ephemeral
as the powder
of a butterfly wing.
A wind-blown apple blossom
changes on the way down.
It comes to know
falling
and the fragility
of the air
that once seemed
almost solid.
Sir Isaac Newton was right:
what goes up
does come down.
But the ground
does not end its descent.
It continues into the mystery
below roots.
A thing blossoms
again in the dark
of its unmaking.
And Newton was wrong:
for there is the faint cry
of a bird
in every fallen thing.
Through blue fingers of air
each possibility again
rises out of itself
to populate a new life.

About the Author

Armand Brint's poetry has appeared in many magazines and literary journals over the years. His first book of poems, *Schools of Light*, was published by Linwood Publishers in 1995. Armand has taught creative writing in colleges and universities in the San Francisco Bay Area and in Mendocino County. In 2001, Armand was appointed as City of Ukiah's first Poet Laureate.